A Delightful Little Book on Aging

A Delightful Little Book on Aging

Stephanie Raffelock

SHE WRITES PRESS

Published 2020
Printed in the United States of America
ISBN: 978-1-63152-840-8
ISBN: 978-1-63152-841-5
Library of Congress Control Number: 2019914441

Interior design by Tabitha Lahr

For information, address:
She Writes Press
1569 Solano Ave #546
Berkeley, CA 94707

She Writes Press is a division of SparkPoint Studio, LLC.

To Dean, my forever love

FOREWORD

This is a collection of thoughts about peering over the precipice of older age and deciding to live life as fully engaged as I can. You know why? Because preparing for death has everything to do with how you live life.

No one I know is truly retired, at least not in the way that our parents were. The sixty-, seventy-, and even eighty-year-olds who are part of my life are artists and activists, teachers and entrepreneurs. In the southern Oregon valley where I live, it's not unusual to run into silver-haired folks on the hiking trail or the ski slope. I dance with them at the Friday night dances at our local wineries. I'm blessed to live in a place where older age is just a part of the diversity of the community. Seniors are valued participants. The sign on the Pilates studio where I take class might as well read: MUST BE SEVENTY TO ATTEND.

I'm of a generation that has decided not to go gently into that good night. The results are inspiring and tender. Life has never been so full, and I don't mean with busyness. I mean with intent. The intent of living and loving in great fullness. This is what wisdom is. This is what it means to get older.

We can't transcend aging with some sort of magical formula, but we can transcend worn-out attitudes that don't lend themselves to making aging a positive experience.

I've written about age a great deal these past few years. My website (stephanieraffelock.com) is filled with posts about the exploration of this new frontier. And while my work has appeared on a lot of different blogs, I've especially written for a site called SixtyandMe.com that gave me the opportunity to explore the subject and also to get feedback from readers about their views on getting older. All that writing brought me to the conclusion that, depending upon your attitude and your ability to adapt, these really can be the golden years. And that's what inspired me to put together this book.

I've divided the writings into four sections that reflect the way I think about aging: Grief, Reclamation, Vision, and Laughter.

GRIEF: Aging begins in grief. Loss and letting go become part of the landscape: youthful beauty, physical prowess, hot monkey sex, and the ability to eat whatever you want fade into memories.

RECLAMATION: Once I realized that life takes things away with one hand, I also noted that she offers something with the other hand. This is what I call "reclamation." Here, in the older years, I've reclaimed the writer in me, the philosopher/poet, the wild woman. What we reclaim redefines us as the years accumulate. My husband reclaimed music. Once, at a crossroads in his younger life, he had decided to finish school rather than become a full-time musician. Now he plays the bass every evening after dinner.

VISION: Vision is birth, rebirth, creation, and recreation. Vision is not a list of goals. It's more like the practice of being so fully in engaged with life that you feel its rapture in the smallest things. This vision of the older years belongs to a wiser, deepened soul, steeped in wonder and delight for life.

LAUGHTER: The final section of this book is about laughter, because there is nothing like recalling the good old days with stories that make us laugh. To be able to laugh at the stuff that once hurt means that we've healed or are healing. Humor is the gentle chuckle of recognition and resolve. And it's laughter that ties everything together with appreciation and gratitude for life.

It's an odd pronouncement to want to be a writer at this stage of my life. It's not like I have decades to develop a craft or a career. I doubt that I'll ever get famous or rich doing it. But writing is for me a doorway into the examined life, a way to express the breadth of emotion I feel, a soul bath that dries the tears of loss and inspires the joy of being alive.

These short posts and articles are like the connective tissue holding my writing dreams together. I'm always working on a novel. Who knows where that will go? But these little articles have been a sweet labor where I get to share my heart and mind with readers whom I may never meet, but whose lives intersect with mine nonetheless. And in that, I am grateful and blessed to have connection with the world through the written word.

The words in this book are about aging. None of us are in it alone. We are moving toward the sunset together, and on that horizon eternity lingers. May we all embrace living fully, with unabashed joy and appreciation for this path of transition.

SECTION 1: GRIEF

Aging begins in grief. At first it's the little losses, as if to prepare us for the bigger ones. Loss and letting go become part of the landscape, and they texture us, refine us, and educate our hearts, growing our capacity for compassion.

My mother had many sides: One minute she was teaching me to knit, and the next she was elaborating the finer points of throwing a cocktail party. She was a fallen Catholic, a divorcée who later married a Mormon. Cocktail Mommy and Mormon Mommy. I liked Cocktail Mommy best. She gave up on the knitting lessons too soon, and though I learned how to knit and purl, she never got around to teaching me how to cast off. That's the part that binds the stitches, giving the piece an edge so it won't unravel. Endings and tying up loose ends would never be my strong suit.

WHAT WE LOSE AND WHAT WE GAIN

The third act is the most exciting place in the story. It's where transformation happens. It's the pinnacle, the high point of the story, the harvest.

A friend of mine is limping into his sixties with a sense of loss: loss of youth, energy, and significance. I understand all that and believe most of us go through a passage where we grieve the younger life we've left behind. As someone who has written for years about the transformative force of grief, I've come to realize that the threshold of loss is only the beginning of a remarkable journey. It is a journey that must be claimed for oneself, lest we get stuck in mourning what once was.

Here are a few of the things I've lost and gained:

YOUTH: My skin will never be as firm as it once was, and my booty, in spite of my best effort to keep it perky with exercise, is sagging anyway. The attractiveness of youth gives way, however, to a deep and unwavering acceptance of the circle of life. Every single wrinkle and line has been earned, a face map that says where we've been and how we've weathered the journey. Aging invites us to grow into a deeper beauty: it's no longer the smile on our face as much as it is the expression of our heart.

ENERGY AND PRIORITY: When I retired, every volunteer board within a twenty-mile radius came at me like a heat-seeking missile. I learned quickly that I had to choose carefully what I invested in because I cannot do it all. A waning energy has helped me prioritize what is truly important. The intentions of the heart are still as strong as ever, but the energy in the body is changing. This is a good time to journal about what is truly important in this part of your life. Get clarity. My list is short: time in nature, hiking with Hubby and dog, writing every morning, and preparing one great meal a day that uses as many fresh things from the garden as possible.

SIGNIFICANCE: This one is on us. It's true that we are not as valuable a consumer as we once were, but that's the only significance that we lose. We reclaim our significance when we create a conscious vision for our sixties, seventies, and beyond. What gives us a sense of purpose? What is fulfilling and satisfying? What's on the bucket list? What is truly important for the remainder of my life?

THE TRANSFORMATIVE FORCE OF GRIEF

As we grow into older age, the list of inevitable loss and disappointment grows too. Resist grief and you get stuck. Give her too much attention and she'll eat you up.

Human beings tend to most deeply bond over shared stories of broken hearts and retrieved pieces. Each time I sit with my grief, it teaches me something. And that's the transformative force that pushes this messy, awkward, wonderful life toward greater love and fullness.

THERE'S A TIME AND A PLACE: Ecclesiastes reminds us that "to every thing there is a season, and a time to every purpose under the heaven. . . ." So doesn't that mean that there is a time to celebrate and a time to grieve?

THE LOTUS GROWS FROM THE MUD: Nature is rich with metaphors. The lotus plant roots itself in dark mud. Beauty and compassion are born from grief. Why, then, do we seem to hold it back, especially when it shows up as the unfinished business of healing?

PERMISSION TO GRIEVE: No one in this world escapes grief. Yes, it's present in death, but grief is also the little losses that pile up over time. Friendships end. Children move away. The role of work or career that once defined us is relegated to memory. In these instances, grief can reveal itself as melancholy, angst, or unexplainable tears. If we run from what is asking to be felt, is it any wonder that we are a nation preoccupied with psych meds? Is grief a negative emotion? I don't think so. Mostly, we turn our face from grief because we are not well versed with being in its presence. It requires us to sit still with suffering and be its witness.

WINTER'S DESCENT: For me, winter is the great descent. I'm prone toward the disconcerting rumble of low-grade depression this time of year. I'm also more likely to be quiet and reflective, figuring out things about my writing, my life, and myself. It's the Persephone myth playing itself out, and each year since I realized that, I weather the assault of the dark a little bit more easily. I've come to respect the place where emotions are just under the surface of my skin, bringing me closer to the vocabulary of my heart.

EVERYONE KEEPS SECRETS: You don't need a PhD to see that the personas we craft for social media are all rainbows and unicorns. It's as though the struggles of our lives are shameful and must be kept secret. We need places (probably not social media) to give air to what it means to be human. Too much energy convincing everyone of how positive you are while holding sorrow in abeyance can turn a person numb.

NO APOLOGIES FOR GRIEF: The deep psychic dive into what hurts is liberating. We should all take a little more time to cry and wail, allowing tears to baptize us into fresh starts and new beginnings. No apologies are needed for doing your personal work in the dark. Hang a DO NOT DISTURB sign on your door and know that nurturing a deeper understanding of grief grows us into better, more compassionate human beings.

ADVOCATE FOR THE AUTHENTIC: I am more interested in keeping it real than I am in any preconceived notion of what it means to be positive. In fact, I'd like to kick the whole "positive only" movement in its little ass and shout to the world that we are connected by our shared experiences of sorrow and longing.

The Size of a Parakeet's Heart

I've rewritten my history in a way that helps me to find acceptance, forgiveness, and gratitude. It's not that I changed the facts, but I did change what the facts mean.

Breakfast happened in a sunny corner of the kitchen on a plastic tablecloth. Its flowered print had faded in spots from the sun and the plates that scraped across its surface. The table was pushed against the windows and looked over a struggling garden in which I had once planted the watermelon seeds saved from a late summer afternoon. When the green shoots found their way up into the light, turning into vines, I imagined opening a watermelon stand and selling pieces of fresh watermelon to all my neighbors.

My enterprise was cut short, however, when something ate the vines, shredding their leaves into skinny little pieces.

My mother kept a row of potted geraniums on the table. Red flowers bloomed almost year-round in a world that was mostly bright colors and sunshine. Part of that brightness was Penny. She was my first true love, my first true friend, a parakeet dressed in exotic green, accented by dark veins of blue feathers. Each morning, my mother would open the door to Penny's cage, and the little bird would fly a couple of times around the room, lighting on the table in front of my breakfast plate, chirping while she waited for me to feed her bits of unbuttered toast. Sometimes she would hop onto my shoulder as I ate.

Every day when I got home from school, I checked to make sure that she had birdseed and clean water. I wasn't allowed to let her out unless my mom was there, but I gave her what felt like a lot of my six-year-old attention, crooning, whistling, and singing to her. During the times she was free to fly around, she would always make her way to me, resting upon my hand and hopping up and down the length of my arm. We had our own special way of telling each other "I love you."

One day, my mom and I came home to the smell of paint. I knew the landlord was having all the kitchens in our row of duplexes painted. We had shopped the week before for new dish towels and pot holders to go with the freshly painted kitchen. I hadn't realized that the paint would smell so bad, and I held my nose as I went to check on Penny. But something was wrong. Penny wasn't moving. She sat motionless on her perch, with her head resting inside a bell that hung off of the mirror in her cage.

"Penny?" I shook the cage and she fell. "*No!*"

I heard my mother's sad voice as she rushed to see what was wrong. "Oh, Penny," she said. "I'm so sorry."

"What happened to her?" I asked.

"I think the paint fumes were too much for her," she said. "The painters didn't think to put her cage outside, and she died."

No one in my life had ever died before. I knew other children who'd told me that their grandma or grandpa died, or that their dog died, but I didn't understand what it meant. Something pierced my heart, a feeling of absence so fierce that my whole body hurt.

"I didn't get to say goodbye," I said.

I wasn't sure where Penny had gone, only that she wasn't in her bird body anymore. My mother helped me give Penny a funeral, wrapping her in a scarf and burying her in the garden outside the kitchen window. I marked her little grave with rocks that I placed in a careful circle around the newly turned earth.

For days, I tried to cry the ache away, and then one day the loss no longer consumed me. Eventually we put up the new dish towels and pot holders. We moved to another duplex, another apartment, another town. The years between

Penny and me grew wide with the passing of time. Now, as my hands and feet begin to wizen, I recall this story and write it down. I still have tears left for Penny and the life lesson that she imparted. Love, even the size of a parakeet's heart, is eternal.

LONGING MEMORIES

I don't mind being older. I relish the striving for self-honesty and awareness that comes with revisiting the past. Life is essentially good.

The sound of a chair scooting against the worn linoleum and the creak of the floor against Julia's shoes break the spell. I can smell biscuits and coffee, and I get up from where I am playing in the warm place by the stove to sit down at the table, where I'm given a biscuit that steams when it's pulled apart. Julia's shaking hands add butter to the smooth open surface, along with a tablespoon of preserves made from summer berries. She is old, and I am not. I am a girl of eight. Julia pours me a cup of coffee, half of it milk. For a moment, I don't think about being dropped off here again, about being left again. I'm content with the tastes of her winter kitchen.

Years later, when I remember her, her love still speaks to me in the small gestures of melting butter and coffee that is half milk and in the fire that is kept going so we wouldn't be cold. She was never someone who cuddled me or talked to me, but she smiled when she carefully stepped over the house I'd made out of pillows in front of the pot-bellied stove and softly said, "Yes, yes, yes," as if I'd somehow delighted her.

I dig and rut through these memory places sometimes, embracing the sorrow and its meaning, savoring the sweetness of the love in Julia's yeses and my grief at those days gone by. I used to fear these recollections, but now I count them as blessings. All that changed was an understanding of what it took for cold hands to roll out dough on a floured sink board in the early dark of day. Life has always been this good.

The shadow that invited me back here loosens its grip on the ghost of confusing emotions: a small child left in a farmhouse that sits in the vastness of prairie and sky. I taste again the feelings of the time, so grateful to have remembered. I rip it right from the heart of the matter and keep it close by. This, I tell myself, is the light and darkness that define you.

When the plates and cups sat empty on her table, I saw through the window, light creeping into the day. Snow fell gently on fence posts and dried grasses. I jumped when I heard the sound of a car crunching gravel under its tires as it slowly made its way up to the farmhouse to pick me up.

BETRAYAL OF THE BODY

Becoming a ballerina or the CEO of a Fortune 500 company is probably off the table for good. I'm too old, but it's important to remember, I'm not dead yet.

Occasionally I see a news story about the seventy-something woman who is still pushing weights around a gym. Good for her, but my own connective tissue isn't that thrilled with weights, and the indicators are injury and pain. The physical prowess of youth has receded into the past. I've become like the old car that needs time to warm up and can't be driven as fast or as hard as the newer version.

I knew things had changed irrevocably for me one day when I was enjoying a walk with Hubby and some friends. I spied the small park as we looped around the lake and the trail came to an end. I saw monkey bars. I don't know what got into me. Something about those monkey bars jarred the memory of a barefooted little girl who swung from bar to bar, two, sometimes three bars at a time. In the kernel of that recollection, I could feel it all over again. I ran toward the monkey bars, climbing the few short rungs of metal ladder and placing my hands in position. In my body, I could feel exactly how it was supposed to be—was going to be—then I swung to the right. In reaching for the next bar, I fell on my ass. As I brushed off the dust and humiliation, Hubby rushed to my side.

"What were you trying to do?" he asked.

I didn't answer his question—at least not out loud. I answered for myself, though: *I was trying to be young. I wanted to be a kid again, but my body betrayed me.*

It's sad that life recedes from us in this way. Just about the time we get our thinking straight, the body starts to break down. Each winter when I go by the skating rink, I remember gliding across the ice in bliss. The bounce-back factor from injury is far less than it used to be, and because of that, I won't risk a fall. So I don't skate anymore, and I miss it. That our physical bodies undergo this change where we are limited is a loss, and it's one that we should honor before we move on.

This time of life is fraught with so many different types of changes, and the physical changes that happen to us are more pronounced. Here's a template for how I am negotiating these times and finding new ways to stay physically connected.

GRIEVE AND HONOR THE LOSS: It's okay to lament the loss of the active woman that we were in our twenties, thirties, and forties. Lament the unwelcome weight gain of menopause that may never go away. Go ahead and mumble under your breath that getting old is a pain in the booty. One of life's great truths is that everything changes and ends. As our physical body gets older, we have to find new ways to move and celebrate it. A little indulgence in the sorrow of what is gone before finding our new footing can help us make peace with the changes.

KEEP MOVING: The great, unsung exercise of my senior years is walking. I've fallen in love with it. I now have the time to put on a pair of hiking boots and head up the mountain. I may be slower than the younger part of the pack, but I still make it to the top. No mountain trail? Walk in the town where you live. My friend Dami calls this "urban hiking." Walking everywhere has so many health benefits and doesn't require anything but a decent pair of shoes.

AGE-APPROPRIATE EXERCISE: I rolled my eyes when I wrote that heading. The age-appropriate part does apply when it comes to finding lifelong practices. (Sigh.) Yoga, Pilates, and stretching classes are great options at this stage of life. They emphasize breath, the release of tension, and core strength. They are slow, deliberate, and focused. I find that this type of exercise also calms my monkey mind.

DANCING: Folk dancing, drumming circles, line dancing, tap dancing . . . there are dozens of different types of dancing to choose from that will get your heart rate up and your body moving. Classes for seniors are easy to find at rec centers, the YMCA, churches, and community centers. And it's a plus that you get to share the joy of dancing with your fellow hoofers. Dancing is something you can do in your living room too. My husband and I still love to dance to old Motown. I will never get tired of The Temptations or The Four Tops.

COMMITMENT: Whatever the body is able to do in terms of movement, stick with it and do it often. "Keep moving" is the rule of the day. Walking is my main exercise. Around that, I build other things. Pilates two times a week, and in the summer months, I take the water aerobics class at the rec center pool, which is fun, refreshing, and relaxing.

BE TRUE TO A SPIRITUAL PRACTICE: The body eventually falls away. If we sit in prayer or meditation daily, we prepare ourselves for the stillness and letting go that will greet us up the road. We were never just our bodies. We have always been consciousness, souls, whatever a person wants to call it—the energy of which we are made returns to that greater energy and merges into all that is. I find that to be a comforting thought. So I stay true to a practice that calms the heart and mind and brings me to a grateful and rapturous stillness.

GRATITUDE: People who know me know that gratitude is my practice and my path. As I move deeper into age, I find that an attitude of gratitude serves whatever I do. I'm filled with appreciation for being able to walk so many different places. I'm thankful that my little town offers so many great classes. I'm grateful to understand and honor that everything changes and ends. With that truth, I know that time is finite and today is the day to get outside and walk in nature. I appreciate that I'm still upright and moving. I have gratitude for the new attitudes that aging brings about.

The Long Road to Mother

⌇

An enthusiastic grief is what pushed my friend forward. The etymology of the word "enthusiasm" comes from the Greek word "enthous," which means "inspired in Spirit."

In November, I use the excuse of NaNoWriMo (National Novel Writing Month) to bang out as much of a draft on a new project as I can. It's demanding. I'm not one of those writers who will tell you how much I love the process. I'm one of those writers who fights with herself every day about word count, plot points, scenes that work or don't work. Truthfully, I'm a train wreck to be around when I am writing. I don't care what's going on in the lives of other people. I only care about cranking out a couple thousand words every day.

But here I am today with something so important burning inside me that I'm breaking away from the work of my novel to tell a different story, a story that is bigger than me and is begging me to write it down. This one's for you, Kitty.

Kitty and I met when we were twenty. I can't tell you exactly how—something to do with a party at the naked lady magazine she worked for, a joint we smoked on the fire escape, and the chocolate cake that kept calling our names. We were at that time in our lives when a person can meet someone and recognize immediately that the person will be a friend forever. I recognized her. We became roommates within months of that first meeting and lived a rich 1970s experience. Our twenties were replete with a house in Laurel Canyon where you could often find a stray musician who had stopped by to play us a new song, a box of grass and rolling papers sitting on the coffee table. Our friends were runners at the music publishing houses and record companies. They worked hard and would grow up to become executives one day, wielding power, arrogance, and self-importance with the best of them. But in the 1970s, we were all just a bunch of kids trying to figure out how to do life.

Dancing until the bars closed. Listening to music. Working on less than four hours sleep and waking up excited about every day. In some ways, it was a shallow but terribly enjoyable existence that only looks good on a twenty-something. And Kitty, well, Kitty was the one I recognized, and she recognized me. So we took time with each other that we didn't take with other people. We took time to learn each other's story and fairly early on, I knew that Kitty was adopted and that she was on a search. Who was her mother? Her father? Why was she given up for adoption? It was a silently painful and unfilled longing that would be somewhat abated by age, marriage, and a child of her own, but a longing nonetheless that was never far from her, the background noise of life that just couldn't be tuned out.

Life happened to us and we happened to life, and here in our sixties, when everything fast-forwarded so much more quickly than I ever thought it would, Kitty found her mother. I would betray her by offering the details of who the woman is or the "why" of all of it, but I can share that Kitty went to visit her. She emailed me a short clip from a video that her husband took of the reunion. Her birth mother is a gentle southern woman holding onto her daughter while crying, "You are mine." Kitty's hand, caressing the woman's cheek, the laughter that escaped from them as a rush of emotions showed on their faces—grief for what had never been and a gratitude for what now was.

This video. Kitty's story. This is what was more important than today's word count on a damn novel. More important than my self-involved surrender to the latest love/hate writing project. This is the happy resolve to my friend's lifetime longing, a story that demonstrates that the power of love is stronger than we ever really understand. The rest of the story? Well, that's for Kitty to tell. And I do believe that she will write it one day. That will be the real conclusion.

To my dear friend, the one who inspired me to write, who is far from home, meeting her birth mother with hugs and kisses, deep understanding, and few regrets. You rock my world, Kitty, and I am so happy for your reunion.

SECTION 2:

RECLAMATION

Life takes things away with one hand and offers something with the other hand. This is what I call "reclamation." What we reclaim redefines us as the years accumulate. Did you leave a musician, a writer, a wild woman behind? Reclaim that part of yourself now. Pull her close and whisper that you won't leave her again.

In my first writing class at UCLA extension, I was terrified that I might have to read something I'd written aloud. I worked for a production company filled with real writers who all had MFAs. My job was to type for them, but I wasn't one of them. They were well-groomed flower beds, the kind that people slow down to look at when they are driving through an expensive neighborhood. I was the brash yellow mustard seed that grew in vacant lots next to old tires and beer cans. I was the wild weed between concrete sidewalk slabs. You can yank it out by its roots, but it always comes back. It's back now. I deliberately reclaimed it, and I think it's beautiful . . .

Reclamation

In my heart lives a sassy, sensitive, and bare-footed little girl who understands that life is all about surrendering to the experience while you learn to dance with it.

Stand as a spiritual warrior at the threshold of old age. This is no time to shrink away, to believe the lies of insignificance or uselessness. Do not retreat or retire from the world. Instead give yourself to your passions and your dreams. This is a time of great fruition, blooming, and moving closer to the source of our creation.

GATHER WHAT'S BEEN LEFT BEHIND: A friend of mine recently wrote about her short story being published in a prestigious literary magazine. She is seventy-four years old, and, though a writer for all those years, like many of us, life intervened. Marriage, kids, work, the tragedies and celebrations of family life consumed her. So when her short story was accepted by this magazine, it was a *Velveteen Rabbit* moment for her. She felt she had become real, a real writer. Into herself, she had pulled back and reclaimed a lifelong love of storytelling.

THE JOURNEY TO RECLAIM: When I read what she had posted about her journey, I wept. She'd written a story about being published for the first time at the age of seventy-four. I was filled with enthusiasm for her and deep inspiration for myself. It had nothing to do with her age and everything to do with her passion. She was living out loud, fully, completely, giving herself to her art, and I was inspired to want to live that fully too. Isn't that what we all want as we grow old? To live life fully and passionately, sharing our stories, our music, our art, our gardens, all the different things that we love about life for as long as we can?

My husband, Dean, grew up playing bass trombone. Later, he played the bass guitar. Now that he is semi-retired, he has given in to the pull to study music theory. He's currently taking an online course with the Berklee College of Music. He plays and practices his bass every evening after dinner, losing himself in music that beats to the rhythms of his heart. He has reclaimed something left behind, and it is richly nourishing his existence.

FIND WHAT NEEDS TO BE RECLAIMED: My friend reclaimed her passion for writing. It had taken a back seat in the years that she was there for her family. My husband reclaimed his love of music, also something that had taken a back seat to marriage, mortgage, and a career. This is the great joy of aging. You get to do art for the sake of art, commit to a standard of personal excellence. What is reclaimed gives us a new and fresh life. Each person can and should decide what she wants to gather back to her now. Life has shifted, and we can reclaim those things that were cast aside when we were raising kids and paying our way.

ART AS WORSHIP: We pay homage to Creation by what we create. When our life has ceased to be about the identity of work, family, and accumulation, we are left with the worshipful state of making music, making art, making stories, making crafts, and making gardens. These things are not done with the mind that created our work or our careers. These things are brought to life from our hearts and our souls.

DO NOT LAMENT: Many are the times that I wished I'd come to my writing earlier in life. But like all of us, life had her way with me, and I write today *because* of the varied experiences of living this long. Had I taken another path, I might have been someone who did not feel the burden of stories pressing against her heart, seeking release. Seems I must remind myself again and again that the fullness of life can't be found in the past, but rather in this present moment where I can give myself fully to something so that I, too, have that *Velveteen Rabbit* moment. I am real.

We should stand proudly in our years and not lament. This is the time to live life in a sacred way, to reclaim those things once thought of as lost. Pick up the pen, the knitting needles, the paintbrush. It's time to give ourselves fully to the life we make. Let passion be the wind that lifts our wings.

Note to Myself
on Creativity

This is a great time to immerse in our passion, be it an art form or a craft like sewing or knitting or words on a page.

I've had a rebirth and reclamation of my creativity. My dream of being a writer had long taken a back seat to marriage, mortgage, and business—life's interventions on the road to responsibility.

Writing has been my love since I was a teenager. It was a way for me to figure out feelings and experiences and make sense of them. In every other part of my young life, I was a poor communicator, but when I wrote, I knew how to tell the truth. So at sixty-two years old, armed with a reclaimed desire and a dusty degree in creative writing and poetics, I sat down and wrote my first novel. It wasn't a good novel, but I wrote the whole damn thing and proved to myself that I could. As soon as I was done, I turned right around and wrote a second one.

Just as suddenly as I'd found myself on my ass under the monkey bars, I now found myself soaring with a creative burst of energy beneath my wings and felt more alive than ever. Getting older presents a clear and simple choice: you can resent what life takes from you and miss what life is presenting, or you can let go of what is past and embrace the gifts of the harvest.

Things to Get Rid of and Things to Embrace

The real priority, the real greatness of these years is not in accomplishments but in the ongoing conversation between hearts.

As the end of the year approaches, I begin to putter around in closets and cabinets, donating those things I'm not using. I enjoy simplicity and orderliness. But it's not just the cabinets and drawers that deserve attention, it's the things in our psyche that we are willing to give up. The cycle of life is a wondrous shedding of old skin and getting comfortable in the new skin. This is an invitation to think about what worn-out things need to be retired at the end of this year and what things need to be embraced.

When I turned sixty-five, I got rid of a lot of stuff. I got rid of a lot of clothing and a box of hair dye. Those things were designed by someone who thought that I should be pulled in, pushed up, squeezed together, balanced when I walked, and—oh yeah—have different colored hair. And yep, I bought into it. When my husband moved from full-time work to the part-time, semi-retirement that we now enjoy, I got rid of the things that were someone else's idea of how I should be:

DREADED PANTYHOSE: Any leftover pairs of pantyhose that I had hiding in the drawers, I axed. I hope that whoever invented these sausage casings of the late 1960s has to spend time in a pair in purgatory.

HIGH HEELS: Every last pair of bunion-producing, blister-inducing high-heeled shoes that I'd saved, thinking one day I would wear them to a Christmas cocktail party, were replaced by something flat, warm, cozy, and wide. People in my little valley wear warm flannel shirts when they gather, and no one gives cocktail parties anymore, do they?

BAD BRAS: I wanted to burn all my underwire bras, with the tight, nasty, cutting straps. But, they don't actually burn. I know. I tried once in 1969 by ceremoniously placing my bra in a trash can and lighting it. It kind of melted, but it didn't really catch fire.

THONGS: Does this even need an explanation?

HAIR DYE: I worked with my hair stylist so I could stop dying my hair. Now it's turning silver. I prefer the word "silver" over "gray" because silver sparkles, and I think that women our age sparkle.

And here are some things I've embraced:

LAUGHTER: A commitment to spend more time laughing. Any old comedy with Robin Williams usually does it for me. A glass of wine and chocolate can definitely enhance the experience.

TEARS: Permission to spend more time crying. We don't let ourselves cry nearly enough in this culture. We judge it as negative or unnecessary, or we're ashamed. Forget that! Tears are cleansing, soothing, and releasing. A good cry can give you a sense of tenderness and openheartedness or a much-needed sense of release.

WALKS: More walks with friends. When I worked every day, I sometimes met friends for lunch. It was convenient and a way to connect. These days, I'm able to invite friends for an early morning or late afternoon walk. The goal is still to connect, but to connect in a place where we get some good exercise and are surrounded by nature. Oh, and I haven't given up on lunches, either.

VOLUNTEER: I didn't have the time to volunteer during my office days. These days I do, and, as a result, I've met wonderful people who share similar interests. I get to feel good about giving my time and energy to a worthy cause. Giving provides a balance to my life, reminding me how fortunate I am to have good health and love.

What we shed are the "things" that gather dust—the things that bind, the things that have become clutter. The new skin is made up of the intangible—purpose, meaning, connection, joy, and love. It's really a pretty good trade-off.

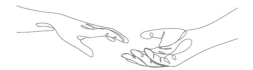

Ageism and the Fitness Clothing Industry

Tight skin and injected lips aren't nearly as sexy as the seventy-something who still goes to the gym every day and works it.

*P*retty much everyone recognizes the benefits of exercise. An entire industry has been built around promoting proactive health. You can see it in our food and drug commercials, both of which emphasize diet and exercise. But the companies that promote exercise the most are the fitness clothing lines, companies like Athleta, REI, and Lululemon. These companies have been great in showing us inclusiveness with a diversity of body types, ethnicities, moms, and kids, but if you are over sixty, evidently you don't exercise—or at least that's what the ads portray.

I've been a loyal Athleta buyer for more than thirty years. I still wear their leggings and tops to my Pilates and yoga classes. In my little town, those classes are densely populated by women over sixty. The women of a certain age I know hike, row, take fitness classes, ski, camp, and bike. Why then are we not part of the message that fitness benefits everyone, not just the young? Why are we not represented in this line of athletic wear?

THE CORPORATE MESSAGE: I don't count if I'm over sixty. I can't exercise. I can't be fit. I'm no longer a real athlete, and therefore I don't deserve to wear stylish clothing. Okay, maybe it's not that harsh, but we all know that the attitude exists and is featured prominently in ads that show young women climbing the hills with nary a sixty- or seventy-year-old in sight.

THE QUESTION: For all those fitness clothing companies that aren't using models in their sixties and seventies, what are you afraid of? Afraid your leggings won't sell if you put them on an older woman with wrinkles and gray hair? Afraid you'll lose your sexy edge, because what's sexy about getting older? What if depicting mothers and their kids exercising could grow to include generational exercising? Now *that* would be sexy, and it would be a positive message: keep moving, regardless of your age.

HERE'S WHAT COMPANIES NEED TO CHANGE: The fitness fashion industry needs to ask itself this question: What do you want for your mom and your grandma? Would you really prefer that they sit in a chair and atrophy until they die? Or would you like them to live with as much vibrancy and joy as possible? When I die, will anyone will say, "Geez, if only she'd looked better in leggings"?

WHY I WON'T SUBMIT TO THE AGEIST MESSAGE: I am so proud to be a part of a consciously aging community where people exercise well into their eighties. I may be a little bit slower and a little less cut, but the same values of health and fitness that I held thirty years ago are still true today. And I will vote with my pocketbook whenever possible. I will keep looking for fitness clothing companies that aren't afraid to promote physical activity to seniors. They're the ones that will get my business and my accolades.

You Got
to Have Friends

To have a good friend who remembers the miles shared, who knows me to my core and loves me anyway . . . that's the stuff that's cause for celebrating.

As the years accumulate, the "wash, rinse, repeat" cycle of love and loss quickens in our lives. Our older years are a time when we are more identified and defined by the quality of our relationships, rather than by our possessions or our jobs. Meaning is now found in a sense of community, family, and connection.

Bette Midler sang it best in "You Got to Have Friends." Friends are a choice, whereas family is a given. Friends allow us to express love for humankind. They can be, at their best, validation for our dreams, support when we fail, and celebration when we win. In other words, they walk through life with us.

As we get older, we're aware that the potential for loss rumbles just under the surface at all times. This, for me, is the driving force that makes me want to love fully, as tomorrow may not bring another chance. The loss of a friend seems to take a little bit of our energy away when they leave. So the question becomes, do we withdraw or do we continue to risk new friendships?

LONELINESS: It is a part of the human journey to want to belong to some place, to someone. Loneliness is the worst illness, the worst diagnosis a person can have at any age. It is the illusion of not belonging. Friends ease that ache, helping us to find joy because we are designed to function best with human interaction. To care about someone beyond yourself is a fulfillment of our shared destiny.

Solitude is different. Solitude is deliberate, a sacred space for reflection and enjoying our own company, but that's not what I'm talking about here. Loneliness can eat us up and sentence us to life without meaning. Relationships are a crucial component of a balanced life. So how do we make new friends throughout life when we know the years of loss and letting go are upon us?

THE QUALITIES OF BEING A GOOD FRIEND: Everyone has criteria for friendship. Mine are to be the kind of friend I would like to have. This provides me with an ongoing ideal and practice.

- Share your *joie de vivre*. The French phrase means an exuberant joy of living.
- Practice saying "please" and "thank you" about everything.
- Listen without interruption. We all want to feel that what we have to say matters and that someone cares. The quality of listening is one of the great gifts that we give to friends.
- Avoid gossip. Even though, I confess, it can be rather delicious to dish about who screwed up and how, those conversations never lead to any kind of bonding or deepening of connection. Worse, they usually hammer us with regret later on.
- Share the things you love: movies, books, a good meal, a perfect cup of tea, walks, music, crafts. Find common ground and enjoy it together.

ENGAGE IN COMMUNITY: Being active in your community means putting yourself out there and inviting people into your life. I sit on the board of the university library in my town. The board is an intergenerational mix of student representatives, middle-aged professors, and community members who, like me, are over sixty. My contact with this group on a regular basis exposes me to young ideas and scholarly minds, and offers a space to contribute and share my own hard-won wisdom. Volunteering for a cause in which one believes is just one way to keep making friends in a community.

OLD FRIENDS: There are those with whom we share history. Staying in touch keeps them in our hearts. I've done a couple of big moves around the country in my lifetime, leaving close friends behind. But in this digital age of Facebook, emails, texts, and cell phone calls, it's easier than ever to stay in touch. Friends who were roommates, whose weddings I was part of, who cheered me on when I went back to school— they are a special tether to a cherished past. They remind me of where my journey started and how far I've traveled.

One of the great joys of growing older is to participate in an ongoing invitation and welcoming of those we meet along the way. While some are just a glancing encounter, others become friends. Love *and* loss remind us that we are not alone but share a commonality. We are human beings and belong to the citizenship of this spinning planet, hurling through space and time, growing ever closer to where we began, in the ultimate and gentle friendship of creation.

The Power of "No"

I recently purchased a magnet for my refrigerator that has a picture of a 1950s woman on it, along with the following phrase: "Stop me before I volunteer again." It's my favorite new thing.

Why do I say "yes" to every invitation? Why do I find myself stressed and then realize that I created that stress by overscheduling? My type-A personality tends to cringe at the idea of unscheduled time. Even in my mid-sixties, I'm still goal oriented. Part of that is good. I have a sense of purpose about getting up every day. Then again, *always doing* is not a beneficial way to live life fully, so I've had to train myself in the art of saying "no."

FAMILIARIZING YOURSELF WITH THE "NO" WORD: Invitations to sit on the board of nonprofits, libraries, and organizations that interest you are rewarding and validating. The same with volunteer work or political activism. It feels great to give something back to my community . . . until I accept too many invitations and find myself stressed or overwhelmed.

Or how about those lunches and outings with friends? I have the opportunity for coffee, lunch, or a hike almost daily. I cherish all those invites, but I cannot accept them all. So how to say "no"? If, in my gut, I feel tired and already spread too thin, here's what I try to do: Put my lips in the form of an oval. Place my tongue behind my teeth and make an *n* sound and then add an *o* to it. Finish the sentence with "thank you." Now repeat, "No, thank you." Here's the thing: if I say no to that board position or lunch date, I have to believe that the world won't end, and it won't be the last invite that I ever get.

WHY "NO" IS IMPORTANT: When I say no to some invitations and leave spaces in my day, it means there is time for rejuvenation. Rejuvenation can look like a long, hot bath, a solitary walk in the park, sitting in the sun and watching the squirrels, enjoying a cuppa and writing in your journal, taking a nap. These spaces give us time to process and integrate the events and experiences in our lives. Without these open spaces, we tend to become scattered and even a little frantic.

TIME TO REFLECT: When every minute of my day is not filled, I have time for reflection. The world is a noisy, complicated place, and between the speed of life and the hustle, it can take bites out of my heart. When I reflect, I tap into that place that reminds me of what is really important. I like to light a candle in the morning and sit with my cup of tea and just watch the flame. I muse about the important things in my life and the things that I can let go of. And often I am met by a rich swirl of emotion that accompanies the people, places, and things I hold dear.

WHAT I TELL MYSELF AFTER I SAY "NO" COLORS THE EXPERIENCE: I have a friend who never says no, and as a result she has a lot to share about her bad experiences. "Why do you say 'yes,' when you want to say 'no'?" I ask her. Her usual answers go like this: "Oh, I feel so guilty if I say 'no,'" or, "If I don't do it, who else will?"

Positive self-talk can be important after having a difficult time turning down an invitation or otherwise saying no. "I'm proud of myself for saying 'no.' I really feel like one more task would stress me out. I'm happy that I'm taking care of myself by declining that request. Even though I say 'no' to my friend, I still love and appreciate her, and I know she loves and appreciates me."

Saying no doesn't mean I don't care about others; it means I'm a human being with limitations, and I'm willing to take care of myself in order to live a life in balance.

The B. S. Road Map for Staying Youthful

I want to live a life of purpose that sheds the conventional trappings of what society tells us old age is supposed to look like and act like.

I almost wrote "How to Stay Youthful in Your Sixties: A Six-Step Road Map," but from the moment I put those words on the page, something felt off to me. Did I really think it was important for a woman to hang on to her youthfulness in her sixties? Wasn't that like telling them, "Look, you're friggin' old, and there is no value in that, so here's how to stay youthful." Youth: Is it the be-all and end-all of a woman's life?

The truth about youthfulness is that it is a tiny spot in the rearview mirror of my life. Sagging has set into places that I didn't know could sag. The skin under my arms has become a veritable sail. My graying hair has, for some reason, taken on a texture and life of its own, causing it to sproing. Any woman with gray hair knows exactly what *sproing* means. And don't get me started on the sudden need for digestive enzymes! All these things are the outward manifestations of aging. Is making them go away really what I need to feel important in my life? Certainly the people on Madison Avenue would like to tell me that it is.

Maybe the title I was searching for and wanted to write was "How to Stay Truthful in Your Sixties: A Six-Step Road Map." What would that look like?

PURPOSE: My neighbor Austin is in her eighties. She's a little wobbly at times, but she still climbs the hills around where we live several times a week. When Austin isn't pumping up the inclines, she's making art. Recently she built a small studio on her land, complete with a garage door that allows her to open up her space to the garden when she is working.

Austin has purpose in her life. Her hair is white, her hands bony and veined. She has beautiful hands—hands that know the wisdom and wonder of making art. We all need a purpose, something that makes us feel excited to get up for each day.

RELEVANCE: My husband and I have old Nordic skis. I remember the Christmas we got them. All new and shiny. Couldn't wait to get them out on the snow.

As the years went by, we found ourselves skiing with people half our age who wore little skate-skis and blew past us as we did the Nordic trudge. I laughed and said to Hubby, "Look at us, honey, we're getting old."

He replied, "You gotta keep moving to be relevant."

That statement is not only true in exercise, but it's true in things that develop around us. For instance, I did not grow up with a computer. I was the last person in my state to get email, but I have learned to keep up with what is relevant. Thirty years ago, I would have sent a paper copy of my article to a magazine or newspaper, and now I simply email it. Relevance. Stay up on what's changing in the world.

INSPIRATION: A woman who has made it into her sixties, seventies, or eighties gets some automatic cred for living that long. I did more than a few things right and more than a few things wrong. Now I get to stand in the light of my truth and share my lessons with the world around me.

At the same time, I never want to be too old to be inspired. I have a writing coach who is half my age. She is my mentor, and, in addition to teaching me a lot about story structure, she has taught me that it is equally important to be mentored as it is to mentor. Allowing myself to be curious, teachable, and inspired by someone else nurtures vitality.

I also have a relationship with a young woman whom I mentor in writing. She's sixteen, and she is curious, teachable, and, I hope, inspired. I like the inspirational balance of both.

EAT THIS, IT WILL MAKE YOU BEAUTIFUL: I came of age in my kitchen, reading Jethro Kloss and Adelle Davis, authors of *Back to Eden* and *Let's Eat Right to Stay Fit*. Though I have explored many diets over the years, I always return to the teachings of these two health food pioneers. Their simple diets make sense in terms of staying balanced. They go like this: Eat a lot of fresh, raw or lightly cooked vegetables. Eat lean protein. Avoid processed carbs like crackers, breads, and chips. Eat minimal fruit and stay away from sugar. Drink lots of water.

This is a good diet at any age, but it is especially relevant (there's that word again) as our bodies get older.

Here's what I know: the biggest chemical reaction that happens in the body comes from the food we put in our mouths. Foods either create inflammatory chemicals or anti-inflammatory chemicals. Those chemicals in turn can and will create pain. An alkaline diet that contains a lot of fresh veggies is less inflammatory than a carbohydrate-based diet.

Throw in some good fats, too, like coconut oil and avocado.

I pretty much live off of soups and salads. I enjoy my time in the kitchen, creating my kind of art.

SAY "NO" TO AGEISM: We live in unprecedented times that afford us the luxury or the curse of living thirty years beyond our retirement. Our Boomer generation was built on the back of social change and activism. This is the perfect time in life to be an activist. We can educate those around us to the truth of aging, which is—and should be—that we are human beings first, with the capacity to be well versed in traversing the terrain of the human condition. Our relevance, our significance, is not dictated by an out-of-touch Madison Avenue, but rather by the sense of conscious aging that our generation is uniquely embracing.

GRATITUDE: Every single day that I am alive, I light a candle and I pray a list. It's a big list. I pray thank you. I breathe it in and I breathe it out. I'm sixty-four, and each year I get this sense of how fast it all goes and how we should make the most of every moment regardless of our age.

The body breaks down. Smooth, youthful beauty is replaced by deep and interesting lines, a map that shows where you have been. Pain is a humbling reality, both physically and psychically. Still, the heart does not know age. Go for what the heart says because the essence of who we are never changes.

SECTION 3:

VISION

Vision is birth, rebirth, creation, and re-creation. Vision is not a list of goals. It's more like the practice of being so fully in life that you feel joy in the smallest things. The vision of the older years belongs to a wiser, deepened soul, steeped in wonder and delight for life.

Sometimes I imagine that I live inside a fairy tale as the old woman of the forest, the keeper of the stories. Travelers who have lost their way are drawn to my tree-stump cottage. When they find me, I listen to their tale about being without direction, and then I gift them the perfect story, the one that will help them find their way back home.

FIVE GRATITUDE
PRACTICES

Each day, I get this sense of how fast it all goes and how I have to make the most of every moment, regardless of my years.

I'm struggling with a bit of low-grade depression these days. A combination of several recent events—a friendship that ended, some good old-fashioned family drama, a sense of feeling misunderstood. I suspect others have been through a similar phase. It's the stuff of life. And to that end, we can all get a little down and have difficulty finding inspiration at times.

To feel sick at heart is no different than to feel sick in the body. We have to take the right medicine to restore balance. The best medicine I know of for heartsickness is gratitude practice.

Gratitude practice is a way of opening the heart to appreciation and hopeful possibility. Over the years, I have enjoyed the teachings of Brother David Steindl-Rast, who writes and lectures extensively about the path of being grateful. These ideas for practice are inspired by his work. They are simple and profound.

THE BREATH OF THANKS: Taking full deep breaths slows everything down. I close my eyes and breathe deeply ten times. With each exhale I say to myself, "thank you." I notice that my shoulders will start to drop. My heart rate slows. Studies have shown that a person can actually lower their blood pressure several points with deep, deliberate breathing. And isn't "thank you" a beautiful prayer to whisper throughout the day?

NAMING THE GIFT AND WRITING IT DOWN: Because I am a writer, my office is filled with notebooks and yellow legal pads. When I write down what I am grateful for, it causes me to pause and feel the gift I've been given. I start with three things. I name each gift and write it down. There is something about writing it down that commits the gift in a deeper way into the psyche. One of the things that I wrote down this morning: *I am grateful for this drizzly weather. I appreciate how conducive it is to writing. Thank you for the gift of this gray, calming blanket of mist.*

OBSERVATION: After deep breathing, I let my eyes fall upon the things that surround me, whether inside my house or outside in nature. I can always find something to appreciate. I let the object of that appreciation bring a smile to my lips. My dog is curled up on the rug in my office. This fur baby looks at me with his big brown eyes in which there is never any judgment or assessment. Did you ever hear that funny phrase, "I hope to one day become the person my dog thinks I am?" Observing my dog and then feeling how grateful I am for him lifts my spirits.

SURPRISE: Observation leads to surprise. Sometimes when I get stuck and feel like I've slammed against a concrete wall, I practice the element of surprise. For instance, I didn't expect that small brown bird to sit right on my windowsill and watch me wash the pots and pans. I can focus on what a wonder it is that such a small creature would sit outside my window, curious about me. What is it about a small bird that conjures such gentle tenderness? In the moment of such observations and wonderings, I have made myself more alive.

AWAKENING THE SENSES: David Steindl-Rast writes: "How can I give a full response to this present moment unless I am alert to its message?" What are the activities that utilize our senses? Sitting on the back porch, allowing us to see, smell, and feel the nature in our own backyard? Hot tea on a cold morning awakens our taste buds and tickles our nose with its aroma. For me, the thing that leads me to most appreciate my senses is a walk in the woods. Anything that places our attention on one or more of our senses is what makes up this practice. We can be grateful for our sight, our taste, our hearing. Today I am grateful for the sense of sight, which allows me to type my post and see out the window of my office into the yard.

In an attempt to restore well-being and balance, I am more focused than usual on a deliberate gratitude practice. This is the healing balm that never fails to turn things around for me. Part of my practice today was to write this post. It helped me. It helped me acknowledge to myself that life isn't always perfect, fair, or kind, and yet I can always find a way to open my heart with the practice of gratitude.

Ten Surefire Ways to Shake Off the Myth of Insignificance

I am part of a generation of seekers of conscious awareness who will not go gentle into that good night. This is not our parents' retirement.

Recently, I read something on SixtyandMe.com about what we fear most as we age. The conclusion was that we fear insignificance. I've had those moments, too—the fear that I might be done with the best of living. But it's not true. I'm not dead yet, and neither are you.

Insignificance is a myth. Take a stand. Let's get it down to specifics, shall we? Here are tangible things you can do to feel your great, wondrous, and precious significance in this life.

MENTOR: Nothing feels quite as good as sharing your hard-won wisdom with a young person. I mentor a sixteen-year-old girl in writing. I found her through my state writing organization. I get excited when I am teaching her something new. And I get to ask her lots of questions about what she believes and what she thinks. We have a wonderful, vital relationship that gives me a sense of purpose.

MAKE ART: Creating things brings forth meaning. Quilt. Sew. Knit. Paint. Write. Collage. Sculpt. Play music. Make something with your hands. Involve your grandchildren or the neighborhood kids. Celebrate life through creating.

EXERCISE: Can't be said enough, can it? We all need to move as much as we are able. Yoga. Walking. Hiking. Swimming. Pilates. There are certain forms of exercise I can no longer do because I have too much disc degeneration in my lower back, but I can walk, hike, and swim. Moving gets your "feel good" brain chemicals going and gives you a sense of well-being. I love how deeply I breathe during a yoga class or on a walk. It gives me such a feeling of being alive.

APPRECIATE NATURE: Whether it's a backyard, a city park, or a mountain trail, taking the time to walk in nature and say "thank you" for the beauty enriches my heart. Being in nature can heal a lot of what ails us. A place with a lake, a stream, or a stand of trees becomes sacred when I let myself marvel at creation and allow myself to be awed. I am nature too. Everything and everyone is made of the same stuff as the stars. Reflect upon that!

CREATE A GRATITUDE JOURNAL OR A PRAYER JOURNAL: Writing can be a deliberate action of reminding oneself what is good. I knew a woman who kept a daily journal of her prayers. Writing them down strengthened her intimate relationship with the Divine. I have often kept a gratitude journal in a similar way—writing down and recording all the things I am grateful for. Once I start noting what I have to be grateful for, I realize that I'm going to need a lot more than one journal.

MAKE NEW FRIENDS: While this can seem more difficult as we age, there are lots of opportunities that we can create to open ourselves to friendship. The key is, as it has always been, to seek out like-minded people through the activities that we enjoy. Listen, show interest, and be positive about life. Those are among the qualities that make for a good friend. And don't be shy; take the initiative to invite someone out for a cup of coffee or tea.

GET INTO TECHNOLOGY: What an amazing world we live in. When I was twenty-six and working in an office, I was blown away when I got an IBM Correcting Selectric II, the electric typewriter that allowed you to backspace and white-out a letter. Fast-forward forty years, and now I am on Facebook.

I have Twitter and Instagram accounts. I blog. I have emails. I design my online newsletter with Mailchimp. And all that technology keeps me young as well as connected.

MAKE YOUR OPINION KNOWN: Do you write? Share your point of view with your local newspaper through articles or letters to the editor. Blog. Write a family newsletter. It's very satisfying.

WEAR COLOR: Lots of color. All throughout my thirties and forties I had a closet full of black. It was flattering. I could dress it up or dress it down. And along with a pair of high heels, I thought black made me look cool and sophisticated. These days, I wear color. Lots of it. Color makes me happy. I don't blend in; I stand out.

STAND IN THE LIGHT OF YOUR TRUTH: Stand up as straight and tall as you can. Speak up. Shine your passion and purpose in the world and, most of all, educate those around you about aging. It's not the end of something; it's the beginning of the most sacred and interesting chapter of life

A List of Things I Want My Nieces to Know

I trust what my heart tells me because the essence of my life, the soul of me, is what never changes.

There are certain things I want to tell my nieces and my grandnieces before I check out. Maybe they already know. They are all a lot smarter than I will ever be. But along with the title of "crazy old auntie" has come some wisdom. Okay, dear nieces, one and all, here is my list. Take note:

LIFE IS TOO SHORT TO HATE YOUR THIGHS. No one ever got smarter or kinder because of the size of their thighs. Please try to remember that you are a human being and not a chicken part.

LIFE IS NOT AIRBRUSHED. For about twenty seconds when you are nineteen years old, you have perfectly flawless skin and great hair. This is just before you start to age by advertising standards. Screw advertising standards! The lines in your face and on your hands will tell you more about character and substance than unlined skin or silky hair. And trust me, only women in shampoo commercials have hair that silky. The rest of us either have mouse fur or horse manes that no amount of the right shampoo can change. But I digress, so I'll repeat: life is not airbrushed. It's not supposed to be. It's full of flaws, imperfections, and messiness. If your life doesn't contain these three elements, then you are not really living.

LIFE IS NOT NEARLY AS FUN, POLITE, OR SMILING AS WHAT'S POSTED ON FACEBOOK. Social media is not reality. No one smiles that way with their husband, their partner, their boss, or their friends all the time. In reality people sneer, stare, space out, and chew with their mouths open. Be real. Be vulnerable. Be authentic and be yourself . . . and don't waste too much time on social media.

YOUR WEIGHT IS NOT A GAUGE OF YOUR WORTH, AND NEITHER IS YOUR BANK BALANCE. You are a lovable, precious, beautiful woman, and it's the contents of your heart that matters. Assess yourself and others by that single factor—the contents of heart—and you can never go wrong.

DON'T BE AFRAID TO SPEAK UP AND BE FIRST. You don't always have to take the smallest portion or sit in the aisle seat instead of next to the window. Claim the drumstick at Thanksgiving. Don't always tell people "It's okay" when your feelings get hurt. Take the time for self-care. Believe me, your family will not starve or wither away because you took the time to nurture your own self. You don't always have to come last.

NEVER STOP READING. Fill your head and your heart with adventures and history, with fantasy and tales. Learn something new every day. It keeps us young.

DON'T FREAK OUT ABOUT GETTING OLD. It doesn't have to be life's buzzkill. Instead, make sure you eat well—yes, that means vegetables—and get outside and exercise every day. This is what really makes a difference when you push past the half-century mark.

BE A SISTER TO ALL WOMEN. We are alive in a country at a time when women's rights can never be taken for granted. Let's make sure that we always advocate for women's empowerment and commit to helping other women, not judging them.

PRACTICE GRATITUDE EVERY DAY. Life is shorter than we think. We demonstrate that we love life by celebrating it. It's a total cliché, but that's because it's so true: make the time to dance, sing, and, most of all, laugh.

KNOW THAT I LOVE YOU. May your life be rich with love and goodwill, and may you never forget your crazy old auntie. I will keep you close in my heart forever.

WHAT TO DO WITH FAILURE AFTER FIFTY

I dance just as much as I used to. Only now I have to be careful that I don't induce whiplash.

I know J.K. Rowling's story by heart—the young, impoverished single mother who stayed true to her writing dream in the face of a failed marriage and what she saw as a failed career choice. The urgency of her circumstances turned her desire to write novels into a fierce perseverance that birthed Harry Potter. I wish that I could say my own writing dream arose in me with the same clarity, but I'm like a Christmas cactus—a houseplant that only blooms in the brittle cold of winter. I did not come to novel writing until I was sixty-two.

A year ago, I landed a top literary agent to represent my debut novel, which made me feel that the brass ring was within my grasp. But a couple months ago, the agent sent me a long list of rejections from publishers, most of whom were generous and encouraging with their praise and admiration for my work, even as they said "no."

While framable remarks from top publishers might have inspired the mature professional, I cried my eyes out, questioned my talent, and licked the wound of failure as though it were my last meal.

Failure after fifty feels different than the failure of youth. Even with its many philosophical and moral lessons in character building, it takes on more significance than if I were, say, thirty-two. It's the *lack of time* that creeps into the space and underscores the fact that it's all finite. Dreams and mortality collide, and the unspoken fear is this: What if I die before I see my dream manifest?

There are only two responses to failure at any age. One is to quit. That is the simplest and most seductive of the two. The other is more demanding and requires reflection. In the second scenario, failure becomes the guide that opens the doors to dig deeper into your psyche and keep going. You can choose option two all the way until you really do no longer walk this earth.

If I have learned anything about failure, it's this: I can run into the arms of a good attitude too soon. I need to take some time to mourn my disappointments before I hit the mental reset that makes it all tenable. The mental reset around my failure to sell my novel happened one day when I was still in my pajamas at two in the afternoon, unshowered and taking my sorrows out on a chocolate chip (albeit wheat-free) brownie. I realized that the pain of disappointment I felt was not from the lack of a book contract; rather, it was from not believing in myself.

I looked in the mirror and, after I wiped the chocolate off of my face, saw a woman who could fail spectacularly and keep going. There was no way I was going to stop writing. That seemed a far worse sentence than being turned down by a bunch of publishers. In that moment, success revealed itself. I know who I am—someone whose strivings inform her stories about the transformative forces of grief, failure, second chances, and awakening. This is the very essence of why I write.

Failing is never the final word. It's never the sum total of who a person is. The experience of not succeeding when I feel like time is running out is an invitation to enter the larger vision. And the larger vision is no more complicated than something my mother told me when she was eighty. "Getting old isn't so bad," she said, "but I wish I had left my dancing shoes on a little longer."

I feel so incredibly blessed and grateful for second chances, for unexpected transformations, and for the plethora of publishers who just lit a flame under my feet, sparking my intention to keep dancing. After all, the night is young.

If I should die before morning's light, I will have done so with a heart bursting at its seams with what I know to be joyful purpose. And that is what I consider true success: to find fulfillment in what you do, regardless of the outcome.

Since I'm no savant, I have accepted that, in order be successful, I need failure. I need it because it underscores how important something is to me. And, if I let it, failure will fuel my determination and my focus. I've done more than just eat brownies and stay in my pajamas since I got those rejections. In spite of how miserable I felt, I still got up, closed the door of my office every day, and wrote. There are many things in life that we can't control. The subjectivity of someone's opinion about our work is one of them.

Failure after fifty isn't really *that* much different than failure after twenty, except that we all sweat the time-running-out thing. Maybe that's why I feel so passionately about accepting the invitation to go deeper into the heart of what I love and reaffirm my chosen purpose. I'll either become a viable novelist or die trying. It feels to me like two good alternatives.

A Pack of
Teenage Girls

I always want to ask the question: Am I living life true to my heart?

Walking into the locker room after my swim, I heard them before I saw them—a giggling, chatty pack. Teenage girls. As I approached my locker, I noted that they were everywhere, a veritable pack of locusts taking up space with towels, bikinis, lip gloss, incessant texting and talking. Youthful energy smacking me in the face. I waded through them. "Excuse me, you are sitting in front of my locker. Excuse me, I need to get to my locker."

One young woman, adorable in her black-and-white bikini, also wore a gray wool hat. She stood in front of the full-length mirror, adjusting it as I struggled out of my wet bathing suit and into street clothes. Then I heard her friend say gently, "How are you going to swim if you don't get your face wet?"

Black-and-white bikini pulled off the gray wool hat, revealing a totally bald head. "My eyelashes and eyebrows are beginning to fall out, too, and what if the water makes it worse?"

"Don't worry. You look cute," the friend said.

The swarm of teenage locusts suddenly revealed themselves to be something other than what I had imagined. Six young, kind teenagers who, under normal circumstances, would be overly concerned with how they looked and who they were seen with—because that's the cluelessness of being fifteen, right? Wrong. Oh, so wrong. I bore witness to six young women, one of them obviously dealing with a suffering that no fifteen-year-old should have to deal with, and her friends who had brought her to the pool to swim and who rallied around her with love, support, and protection.

"You look cute," another one of them echoed, and then they disappeared—off to the pool in their little pack.

In an ordinary moment in an ordinary place, I was blessed to experience an extraordinary hope. Sometimes I get cynical and disheartened by this harsh world. I find no inspiration in our leaders who pick corruption out of their teeth from a steady diet of greed and lies. But here, in this locker room at the local rec center, I found hope in a gaggle of teenage girls who are keeping love alive in the simple actions of what it truly means to be a human being.

The Wild Viewpoint
from Childhood

There is no going back to get it right. Truth is, I never really ever figured out life anyway . . . I just made peace with it.

When I was four, my parents divorced, and my father relocated to Glacier National Park, which was a whole different palette of nature from Carlsbad's desert. The change created an interesting phenomenon in my life: what with everyone's angst and all the new beginnings, I became totally unsupervised. A psychologist might call it abandonment, but it's not like I was neglected. I was just left alone, and I learned to make the most of it.

In the winter, in the park where my dad lived, I climbed up the steep hill next to his cabin and rode a sled to the bottom, squealing all the way. In the summer, I loved to watch the rain, warm and pounding, when it unleashed from the skies with a great, gray power and beauty. One day, I got the idea that I should be outside in that rain instead of watching it from a window. No one was around to tell me "no."

Out the back door I went, got on my tricycle, not bothering with shoes, and began riding through the neighborhood, peddling hard through the puddles and loving how the warm water soaked my clothes, hair, and skin. A woman, who also happened to be the local sitting judge, saw me, stopped her car, and demanded that I get in. She put my tricycle in the trunk and drove me to her house, where I was toweled off and given an oversized shirt to wear while my clothes were in the dryer. Then she called my father.

I was told to sit in the living room, where she turned on the television for me. The show that was on was the *Oral Roberts Healing Hour*. Oral Roberts talked about sickness and injury and told the audience to put their hands on the television screen. Then he would yell, "Heal, God, heal!" as though he were talking to a pack of dogs instead of people. I wanted to see what it felt like, so I put my hand on the television screen. As Oral Roberts was yelling, "Heal, God, heal!" and I had my little hand pressed against the screen, my father walked into the room.

He had on his National Park uniform with a plastic thing over his hat that kept it dry. As he looked down at me, he seemed to grow taller. Water dripped off his hat, and he said, "Am I raising a moron?"

I wanted to tell him, "No." Today I would have said, "No, you are raising a wild child," but nothing came out of my mouth that day, and then it was too late. He gathered me up, and we went home. I don't remember being punished. I was probably off into the woods the next day looking for another adventure.

That was my last summer as a wild child. As I got a little older, I became interested in being like other girls. Matching my shoes and belts grew more important than exploring new places. By the time I was seventeen, I was ready to leave home and explore again. Seventeen is way too young to leave home, but having learned self-reliance at such an early age, it wasn't that big a deal. I got into a lot of trouble when I left home, and, just like riding a tricycle in the rain, some of it was great fun.

Remembering this makes me smile. I feel like I'm reentering those wild times. It's not so much a place—the wild—as it is a state of mind. And I'm finally old enough that I no longer confuse recklessness with wildness. Wild is more an authenticity that speaks truth without worrying about what others may think. Wild is the rawness of heart that drinks in the world in all its pain and all its joy. Wild is crying when the full moon rises and the geese fly overhead. I believe that the wild is what will carry me home.

SECTION 4:

LAUGHTER

There is nothing like recalling the good old days with stories that make us laugh. To be able to laugh at the stuff that once hurt means that we've healed or are healing. Humor is the gentle chuckle of recognition and resolve.

In my twenties, I worked as a production secretary for a show called The Midnight Special. One day I got a better job offer. Thinking I was being professional, I typed a formal letter of resignation to my boss, Mr. Sugerman, and gave it to him. I should mention that those were the days before spell-check. What I'd meant to say was: "I am leaving to take a job that will afford me more responsibility." What I actually typed onto the page and handed to my boss read: "I am leaving to take a job that will afford me more reposeability." The letter was circulated among the staff and Mr. Sugerman's friends for a few days. It was a good laugh and partially true. Follow-up note to Mr. Sugerman: I now live a wonderful life of repose.

It's Really
Pretty Funny ...

Life is reinventing us all the time, whether we like it or not.

AGING: It's happening, and it's weird. Some days, I am relaxed in the process of it. Other days, I am Don Friggin' Quixote, battling the windmills with Pilates classes, hiking, and an overabundance of green salads and coconut water.

I've read all the inspirational articles about embracing and celebrating your sixties and your seventies. Hell, I've even written some of those articles, but I have to say, whether I embrace my age or not, it's still weird. It really does seem like twenty-seven was last week and that forty-seven was just yesterday. I have to arm myself with dignity and grace because that, and a sense of humor, is what it's going to take.

DIGNITY: Recently, I attended a charity yoga event where the proceeds went to raise awareness about sex trafficking. After twenty minutes of sitting on the floor, my scoliotic back was screaming mad. And I muttered to myself, "Never again."

Scoliosis, arthritis, brittle connective tissue—those things can alter how one does certain activities. After the event, I went to the director and suggested that next year there be a section for chair yoga. I can do the same breathing and arm motions sitting on a chair without hurting my back. The chairs would have yoga mats in front of them for those who can still do certain yoga poses on a mat. I felt a sense of dignity that I had found a solution that would allow my full participation. That's what dignity means to me—taking care of myself spiritually, emotionally, and physically, to the very best of my ability. Living well is not a given. It must be claimed.

GRACE: Grace is gratitude in action. No one likes being around a complainer. I'm not saying that aging doesn't have a list of legitimate complaints. It does. You don't have to look too far to find aching knees, blurred vision, or bad backs, not to mention sagging skin. Note to self: smiling will make your face look less saggy, so find reasons to do it.

Too tired to take a walk? I hear you. But when we push ourselves to do that walk, achy knees and all, we are going to feel better when we're done. That's the grace of it.

HUMOR: Keep a sense of humor close at hand. Sometimes I catch myself groaning as I get up from a chair. I have to laugh at myself when I do. I have moments when, through my eyes, it looks like only twelve-year-olds have driver's licenses, and they're all in my lane. That's worth a chuckle. I can now speak with real authority about all the different kinds of fiber as if I'm discussing fine wine. That's pretty funny too. The insults of aging can be fodder for laughing our way toward the finish line. Life is going to have its way with us, so we might as well develop a sense of humor about it.

BE THE CRONE: Some women bristle at the word, but it's a word that deserves to be reclaimed by us. "Crone" means crown. It is the crowning glory of having reached a wise age. It is the mark of being an elder. Let's face it, at this point in life, I know stuff. I know more stuff now about what it means to fully be a human being than ever before. I've experienced loss, grief, failure, and pain, and I'm still standing. I know how to hold life's suffering and life's joy side by side. That's why this is such a good time to mentor or volunteer. At the very least, I can use my crone years to write out the things I've learned about living this long. Let's claim our voice and stand in the light of our truth.

Aging is a strange new journey, a time of humbling and a time to laugh, a time to be wise and a time to remember childlike wonder. As a Zen master once said, "This being so, how shall I proceed?"

Proceed with caution. Proceed at your own risk. Proceed with laughter, love, grace, and dignity. Say "thank you" as if it were the prayer of your life.

THE BABY PLANE

The thing that I love most about other people's children is that they're other people's children.

*P*icture this: late evening, and I've been traveling since noon, East Coast time, headed for the West Coast. I feel grimy. Why? Because planes, even if I showered ten minutes ago, always feel grimy. They are long flying tubes filled with people who cough, sneeze, and fart into their seats. When those people get off of the plane, I get onto that same plane and it's one of those wash, rinse, repeat things, but without the wash part.

My husband and I flew from Tampa to Denver and then caught a small regional plane for the last leg of our journey to Oregon. It turned out to be the Baby Plane. I don't mean the plane was small, though it was. I mean the plane's passenger population contained at least four children under the age of two. I know when I see a small child at the gate, that child will be sitting directly behind me. I know this because I have some sort of weird Baby Plane karma with the universe. And last night's flight was a case in point.

I sat directly in front of a young mother holding a squirming, sleepless eighteen-month-old. The kid looked innocent enough, smiling and cooing, pulling herself up to peer over the top edge of my seat and presenting that angelic little face that God gives children so we'll put up with their antics. Then the plane took off, and Sweet Baby behind me turned into the devil's spawn. Her little legs kicked the back of my seat with the gusto of a soccer player as she tried to escape from her mother's embrace and terrorize the other passengers. This kid had a scream so high-pitched that, had there been any glass on board, it would have shattered. Sweet Baby may have a future as an operatic soprano. She certainly has the lungs for it.

Once she started crying and shrieking, the rest of the babies on the plane joined in. It was a regular cacophony of screech and scream, punctuated by the desperate cooing of a handful of mothers, helpless to stop the conspiracy.

My husband said, "You know, I feel just like that."

Me too. If tantrums were allowed for adults, I would have had one, right there in my seat. I would have stomped my feet, whined about the noise, and wailed that I wanted to be home in my own bed, surrounded by peace and quiet. But, like all the adults on the plane, I kept the thought of those actions to myself.

It's hard enough to be a parent and harder still to be a parent on a plane, where you are helpless to control the determination of such a small human being. As the plane landed, all the babies stopped crying. Clearly the whole thing had been planned. They had probably met at the changing table in one of the airport restrooms and plotted their little baby tyranny.

As I waited for our luggage, I saw the young mother who'd sat behind me with Sweet Baby, who was now an angel again. The child looked at me with that cute face, smiled, and rested her head on Mommy's shoulder as they walked away. I was compelled to tell the mom that she was a good mom. Really, I thought she should receive some kind of award for hanging on to a kid whose only objective on that flight was to see if she could burst eardrums.

The proliferation of the human race depends upon women not realizing how all babies have an evil twin just waiting for the right opportunity to come out, which usually happens on planes or in grocery stores. I imagine young women fantasizing about having children and *tsk-tsking* when they see children throwing tantrums in the market. *That will never be my child,* they think. By child number two, when the kid is rolling in the aisles of Safeway screaming, young Mommy will simply step over him to get to the tomato sauce. That's just the reality of parenthood.

It does take a village. Sometimes it is the villagers' job to just endure while conspiring innocents screech and carry on. Chagrined parents do the best that they can. The only acceptable revenge is the mantra that you hear the more experienced mothers utter throughout their child's life: "Just wait until you grow up and have kids of your own!"

JOY TO THE CHOIR

Humor is the gentle chuckle of recognition and resolve, and the great cosmic belly laugh of having experienced it all.

It wasn't fair! For two years in a row when I was in elementary school, Cheryl McAdams got to be Mary and wear the blue veil and hold the Baby Jesus doll in the Christmas pageant. Cheryl McAdams stepped on my feet whenever she could, leaving black marks on my white socks and scuffs on my Mary Janes. When we were lined up, waiting to go into assembly, she would turn around, stomp on one of my feet, laugh, and then turn to the front of the line again like she hadn't done anything. No way should she have been Mary two years in a row!

I sang in the choir, directed by Mrs. Luella Pearson. Mrs. Pearson had bluish-gray hair that she sprayed into a helmet. Her face was heavily powdered. "Like a porcelain doll," my mother said, but I thought she looked more like a powdered donut.

Our school was a private one, a fact that my mother liked to share with relatives in a way that didn't make it private at all. Each year, we put on a Christmas pageant. The local television station invited the school to the studio and filmed the entire thing. It was the big event leading up to our winter break.

In parkas and scarves, boots and mittens, we marched off the school bus by grade, so bundled against the snow and cold that we looked like a little troop of Michelin men. Volunteer parents and teachers took us to dressing rooms, where we were greeted by rows of freshly pressed, neatly hung choir robes. Sizes were found, parkas and boots stashed, and soon each kid was wearing a black robe with a white collar and a big red bow tied under the collar.

Mrs. Pearson inspected us as we stood in lines just the way that we would when we sang. She walked up and down, her heels clicking on the concrete floor, and gave us instruction.

"Be like angels," she said. "Look directly into the camera and smile your best smiles while you are singing. Remember that smiling helps to raise the note so that you do not sing flat."

Hearing these instructions, I vowed to hold the notes dear in the hopes that Mrs. Pearson might notice and cast me as Mary next year.

It cannot be easy for mere mortals to deal with seventy first- through sixth-graders. Our excitement was ramped up by the cookies and candy supplied by the television station. Like fat little puppies at the trough, we practically licked the floor when the sugary treats were gone.

The thing about so much sugar is that it makes kids think of doing things they normally wouldn't do. Leonard, a boy from my class, had already eaten several cookies and quite a bit of candy. He regularly got in trouble at school. Leonard could bring class to a standstill. He liked to put his hand in his armpit and then flap it like a wing in such a way as to make loud farting noises, bringing bouts of laughter. Girls were not supposed to laugh at fart jokes, but secretly I thought Leonard was a very funny kid.

Leonard was running around the television studio with the Baby Jesus doll that he'd taken from the manger and using it as a machine gun.

"Leonard, I told you last week, none of this nonsense! Stop all this fussing now. Do you want to go sit in the dressing room by yourself? Do you?" Mrs. Pearson repeated, bending down and placing her hands on his shoulders. She straightened the large white collar on his choir robe and fluffed the big red bow.

I was standing right next to them, so I saw it all happen. Leonard listened to Mrs. Pearson with an intense look on his face and then a little smile. Mrs. Pearson straightened up and smiled back, just as Leonard let rip a real fart. Loud, rolling, and fragrant. Leonard started to laugh. All the kids around him started to laugh. Mrs. Pearson turned whiter than the powder on her face and grabbed a handful of her helmet hair so hard that we heard it crunch in her grip. For the rest of the day, she had a dent on one side of her head.

Now Mrs. Pearson had to avoid looking at Leonard because whenever she did, he started to laugh uncontrollably, which brought on more laughter from other kids, except for the group of girls that included Cheryl McAdams, in her stupid-looking blue Mary veil. They stood in their little pod and glared at Leonard.

"He is so rude," I heard one of them say.

"My mother would never let me play with him," said another.

"Why would you want to?" chimed in Cheryl McAdams.

Finally it was time for the choir to line up and sing. The adults herded us to our places, and we stood in two neat rows. The kids in the back stood on risers so everyone could be seen. Excitement bubbled over as bright lights shone down, and a big camera focused on us. Mrs. Pearson stood behind the camera and raised her arms to direct our singing. I remembered what she had said about looking right into the camera and singing with a smile on your face.

We sang the *Reader's Digest* condensed version of the "Hallelujah Chorus" first. Then we sang "Away in a Manger." Each time the camera went by, I looked right into the lens and, without really meaning to, leaned slightly forward as I smiled my best smile. What I didn't know at the time is that none of the other kids followed Mrs. Pearson's instructions, so they didn't look right into the camera. They didn't smile, and none of them leaned forward for the camera.

As we came to the end of "Silent Night," I leaned forward a little too far and fell on my face, taking three other kids out with me. It is to the cameraman's credit that he did not follow my descent with his lens—and to Mrs. Pearson's credit that she didn't put another dent in her helmet hair. As I went down, I could hear Leonard laughing uncontrollably.

On Christmas Eve, my mother, my aunts, and some cousins sat in our living room and watched the Christmas pageant on television. My aunts were laughing and calling me a little ham.

I scowled my best eight-year-old scowl and said, "I did exactly what Mrs. Pearson told us to do, and I was the only one."

"You were definitely the only one, sweetheart," said one of my aunts.

With my arms folded across my chest, I continued to watch as the camera caught the beginning of my fall before cutting away. Leonard could still be heard laughing in the background. The screen faded to black and then to our principal, who wished everyone "a very merry Christmas and a good night" with a sick look on her face.

Somewhere in another part of the city, I'm pretty sure that a powdered Luella Pearson, replete with helmet hair, was watching the Christmas pageant, too, and that she was most likely on her third martini.

Eight Guilty Pleasures
for Any Holiday Season

There are no races to win anymore. There is no competition. There is only an inner striving for excellence, a personal best, and a good nap.

I swear to you that I am not a *bah humbug* kind of person. In fact, I love the holidays, and one of the things that I most look forward to is the moment when business slows, relatives go home, and I have hit every bullet point on my Christmas to-do list. On the second of January, I will need to start behaving like an adult again, but for now, I am sharing some of my holiday guilty pleasures.

EAT COOKIES: I love holiday parties. Whether cocktails or church, I always ask myself this important question: Why eat grown-up food when I can eat cookies? Don't I get enough well-balanced, healthy meals throughout the year? I'm not suggesting that I would ever sit in the back of the closet with a box of gingerbread men in my lap. I only ever did that once. My point is this: I have discovered that I can easily wave a cookie in one hand and hold a drink in the other, and people won't judge. They will simply think I'm being festive. Take advantage. This is one of the few times all year that I can eat like this in public.

GRANDMA'S HAVING A TIME-OUT: All year long I fill up my calendar and show up on time. The antidote for this schedule on steroids is a pajamathon: I must stay in pajamas all day, and if I absolutely have to shower, I change into clean pajamas afterward. And I don't worry about answering the door. I'm over sixty, and I don't owe the world an explanation for hanging out in flannel PJs and socks all day.

BINGE-WATCHING: This often-overlooked resource for the art of doing nothing is now available on every computer courtesy of Hulu, Netflix, and Amazon, and is truly one of the great indulgences of the holidays. One program I recommend is *Good Girls Revolt*. On Netflix, all the past episodes of *New Girl* or *Friends* will keep me entertained with marathon viewing. And don't forget Home and Garden TV for a real binge-watching treat.

MINDLESSNESS: This is a new twist on "mindfulness." Instead of being mindful, I simply space out with You-Tube cat or puppy videos. I make sure to laugh out loud to get the full benefit of the mindlessness exercise. Wine is optional.

PHYSICAL EXERCISE: Finger muscles can get neglected all year long. But I have discovered that I can rebuild my finger muscles by turning the pages of my favorite Christmas catalogues, *The New York Times*, *Rolling Stone* magazine, or any other glossy that I can hold in my hands. I recommend stretching out on the couch to do this exercise. While my fingers may ache a little from so much activity, I know that I can stop at any time, place the magazine across my belly like a little tent, and take a nap.

GETTING IN THE MOOD: Taking serious downtime for one's self is not for the faint of heart. Sometimes a woman needs something to help put her in the mood. Here's my list: hot baths, hot showers, home pedicures, good wine, chocolate, and cozy socks.

THE PERMISSION SLIP: If I am still having difficulty with the idea that I am entitled to relax and do nothing, I write a note to myself and post it on the fridge where everyone, especially me, can see it. It looks something like this:

Dear Universe,
Please excuse Stephanie from all the good deeds, respon-
sibilities, and obligations that she usually takes on. Cut
her some slack. She needs a couple of days off and will
return to all the obligation stuff in the New Year.

When the kids and grandkids have gone home, the left-overs have been stored in Tupperware, and the wrapping paper has been recycled, I put my feet up. I deserve it, and I'll be thinking of all the obligations that await me in the New Year as I binge-watch and eat cookies in my pajamas.

Things I Learned from My Dog

Happiness is an attitude of gratitude. I am not quite sure where I first heard that quote, but I can tell you it's what my dog teaches me everyday.

My husband and I live our lives with a goofy yellow Labrador retriever named Jeter. Yes, he's named after the great Yankee shortstop. Jeter is the most unconditionally loving, welcoming, funny member of our family. And in spite of his innate goofiness, he is the ultimate connoisseur of life. Here are Jeter's rules for living a good day:

WHEN YOU MEET SOMEONE NEW, WAG: People translation: Welcome people into your life with smiles, hugs, handshakes, and an open heart.

IF ANOTHER DOG TAKES YOUR TOY, JUST CONTINUE TO PLAY WITH THEM: People translation: Be happy for your friends. Celebrating someone else's successes doesn't mean you won't realize your own dreams.

WHEN YOU'RE DONE EATING, TAKE ALL THE TOYS OUT OF YOUR TOY BOX AND THROW THEM AROUND THE ROOM: People translation: Share happiness, satisfaction, and gratitude with the friends and family that make up your world.

START EACH DAY BY RESTING YOUR HEAD ON THE KNEE OF SOMEONE YOU LOVE: People translation: Begin and end everyday with love and hugs. Cyber hugs count, and so do phone hugs.

EXERCISE DAILY: People translation: Exercise daily. A walk around the block, through the park, or up a mountain will keep us healthy and happy. Stop to smell the flowers. Marvel at the trees and say "thank you." Jeter does.

GET EXCITED WHEN YOU SEE SOMEONE YOU KNOW: People translation: Life is short. Let's share what's in our hearts.

ONE MORE DANCE

It's not just humor that elicits our laughter, it's delight.

The Steiner Ranch Steak House sits on a hill overlooking Lake Travis. A sky streaked with the pinkish-orange tinge of the setting sun relaxed the senses as my husband and I sat at our table in the restaurant's patio. The air was warm and sensual, and a light breeze swirled off the lake. When the sun and the light came to rest behind the wooded hills and lake, the music started. The rock 'n' roll band in front of me was made up of a rhythm section, horns, and a couple of badass women who knew how to harmonize. This is Austin. Music, music, and more music.

By the third song, I was a fan—nodding my head and tapping my foot as our drinks and appetizers arrived. I wanted to get up and dance. Old rock 'n' roll filled me with childlike joy, and judging from the dance floor, I was not alone in that experience.

Hubby and I were enjoying our dinner when I noticed that the hostess was seating an older couple at the table next to us. "Older couple," being a relative term at my stage of life. The man was tall and thin, a bony old dude with a baseball hat that read "World War II Veteran." He had to be at least ninety. He was of my parents' generation, and I felt a lump in my throat thinking about the tremendous sacrifice and nobility of that generation. They just don't make 'em like that anymore.

Once they were seated, the man got up and moved his chair and his place setting so that he was sitting right next to the elderly woman that he'd brought with him. He slid his hand under the table and intertwined his fingers with hers. I'm guessing she was his wife because their connection felt like they had been together forever. She wore a baseball hat, too, only hers had a lot of sparkles and bling on it. My heart swelled when I saw how they leaned into each other a little bit as the band kicked up its next song.

"Oh, my God, they're so sweet," I said to my husband. "I want us to be like that." I'm pretty sure that anyone watching them had that same thought.

About the time I was nudging Hubby to follow me to the dance floor, the older couple stood up, and the World War II veteran led his lady onto the floor.

They proceeded to dance with big grins on their faces, whirling and twirling, raising their arms in the air. They sang along with the words that they knew, and she pranced like a twenty-year-old. There was a little stiffness in her strut, a loss of agility in the careful twirls, but the joy in both their hearts was young and vibrant. The gentleman never took his eyes off of her. He just danced around her, doing his two-step, like he was in orbit and she was the center of the universe. This is what love looks like. This is how beauty redefines itself as we get older.

And it wasn't just one dance. I think they sat out only three or four songs the whole night. During the slow dances, she rested her head on his chest, and he held her tightly, as if they would merge into just one body.

We too often think of older people as frail or feeble. We think that life is over for the ninety-somethings. Yet many more people are living longer and healthier, fully engaged with the world and with each other. When I looked around the restaurant patio, I saw that I wasn't the only one watching them. The old couple had inspired others to lean into each other, to hold hands, to appreciate the love in front of and inside them. I believe that couple gave a gift to all of us lucky enough to bear witness to their dance. They showed us what wringing every last bit of life out of the cloth of our existence looks like.

This is the vision I hold for body, mind, and spirit as I age:

- In body, keep moving, and celebrate that I'm able to move.
- In mind, don't stop relating, learning, or processing the delights of the sensual world.
- In spirit, celebrate and pay homage to life by expressing joy.

These two people are in the winter of their lives, but they have not stopped living or loving as fully as they can. And I don't believe that they will until their last breath. This is the great secret to aging well. Dance on . . . and show the rest of the world how it's done.

Why Is It That We Are Living Longer but Calling Ourselves Older, Earlier?

~

Moving away from the schedule and demands of a career certainly takes away from the stress of life. It's pretty easy at the start of retirement to want to hang out in your sweats all the time. And while one day of binge-watching Home and Garden Television is an awful lot of fun, a steady diet of that kind of inactivity doesn't lead to a good outcome. The old, tired, and somewhat accepted cultural narrative about getting older is that we should slow down. Do that, and offspring will begin to see you as an object of care, rather than an individual engaged in a dynamic process. As Bette Davis once said, "Old age ain't no place for sissies."

Shortly after I retired, I began to miss that little bit of tension in life. It's like strings on a guitar: if they're too loose, they make a flat and uninviting sound, but if they're too tight, they shriek and then break. A little tension is needed to create the tone, to make the music. In other words, challenges and tasks keep us alert and engaged with living.

I celebrate that the Boomer generation is redefining what it means to get older. Aging is a developmental process that can bring spiritual maturation, psychological growth, vitality, and creativity, but we need to work at it.

I hold this season of life as a time where I'm becoming everything that I was ever intended to be—more loving, lovable, creative, engaged, and joyful. I want to live it all. Live it to the very end, with feeling and gusto.

Dear reader, I raise my glass to your awesomeness. I wish you peace, goodwill, and good living.

AFTERWORD

*S*ome of the most enjoyable relationships that I have are the result of people who discovered me through my writing. I love hearing from folks who find something inspirational, wise, or joyful in my work. Reach out to me and say "hi" anytime. Share a snippet of your journey with me. We're all in this boat together, and having made it this far, what a tale we all have to tell. Life is good. Sending you love and goodwill.

Email: stephanie@stephanieraffelock.com

 @StephanieRaffelock

 @Sraffelock

ACKNOWLEDGMENTS

$\backsim$

My very first thank you goes to my best friend, benefactor, and husband, whose encouragement to write has been unwavering. To Jennie Nash, my coach, editor, friend, and teacher, thank you for educating me. To Jenni Egan, Dami Roelse, Geri Hill, and Janet Sontag for being in my corner and sharing the writing journey.

To all the friends and family members who loved me up with encouragement and goodwill: Amy Richards, Geoff Riden, Janet Anderson, Jennifer Coulter, Pat Black, Tom Black, Nancy Picucci, David Raffelock, and Deb Zigler, thank you. And to Taffy and Ross Pelton, I love you for being my champions. Thank you to Kitty and Rob Radler for all the early encouragement. And to Cherill Cliff, my friend from across the pond, who has become a special little light in my life.

To Margaret Manning of SixtyandMe.com, thank you for giving me a space to publish and for being so kind.

To Brooke Warner—you are one hell of a business-woman, helping other women realize their dreams. Respect and admiration! I'm proud to be in the sisterhood of She Writes Press. Thank you.

Larry Brooks and Jennifer Blanchard, I will be forever grateful to you for all you've taught me and for all the ways that you've helped me.

And finally to Mrs. Collins, my seventh-grade English teacher, who helped me to believe in myself at a difficult time—I wish you could know the journey you set me on. I have never forgotten you, and I never will.

About the Author

Stephanie Raffelock is a graduate of Naropa University's program in creative writing and poetics. She interned at the *Boulder Daily Camera* and has penned articles for numerous publications, including *The Aspen Times,* Care2. com, *Nexus Magazine, and The Rogue Valley Messenger, as well as* SixtyandMe.com.

Author photo © Tina Bolling

Selected Titles from She Writes Press

She Writes Press is an independent publishing company founded to serve women writers everywhere. Visit us at www.shewritespress.com.

Flip-Flops After Fifty: And Other Thoughts on Aging I Remembered to Write Down by Cindy Eastman. $16.95, 978-1-938314-68-1. A collection of frank and funny essays about turning fifty—and all the emotional ups and downs that come with it.

The Shelf Life of Ashes: A Memoir by Hollis Giammatteo. $16.95, 978-1-63152-047-1. Confronted by an importuning mother 3,000 miles away who thinks her end is nigh—and feeling ambushed by her impending middle age—Giammatteo determines to find The Map of Aging Well, a decision that leads her on an often-comic journey.

Green Nails and Other Acts of Rebellion: Life After Loss by Elaine Soloway. $16.95, 978-1-63152-919-1. An honest, often humorous account of the joys and pains of caregiving for a loved one with a debilitating illness.

Naked Mountain: A Memoir by Marcia Mabee. $16.95, 978-1-63152-097-6. A compelling memoir of one woman's journey of natural world discovery, tragedy, and the enduring bonds of marriage, set against the backdrop of a stunning mountaintop in rural Virginia.

Renewable: One Woman's Search for Simplicity, Faithfulness, and Hope by Eileen Flanagan. $16.95, 978-1-63152-968-9. At age forty-nine, Eileen Flanagan had an aching feeling that she wasn't living up to her youthful ideals or potential, so she started trying to change the world—and in doing so, she found the courage to change her life.